D1483594

Great Moments in

Olympic
TRACK
& FIELD

By Karen Rosen

SportsZone

An Imprint of Abdo Publishing
www.abdopublishing.com

www.abdopublishing.com

Published by Abdo Publishing, a division of ABDO, PO Box 398166, Minneapolis, Minnesota 55439. Copyright © 2015 by Abdo Consulting Group, Inc. International copyrights reserved in all countries. No part of this book may be reproduced in any form without written permission from the publisher. SportsZone™ is a trademark and logo of Abdo Publishing.

Printed in the United States of America, North Mankato, Minnesota
042014
092014

THIS BOOK CONTAINS
RECYCLED MATERIALS

Cover Photo: Anja Niedringhaus/Robert F. Bukaty/AP Images
Interior Photos: Anja Niedringhaus/Robert F. Bukaty/AP Images, 1; AP Images, 6–7, 9, 13, 14–15, 26–27, 31, 32–33, 37, 38–39; dpa/picture-alliance/AP Images, 10; Press Association via AP Images, 19; Bettmann/Corbis, 20–21, 43; Underwood & Underwood/Corbis, 25; Ron Heflin/AP Images, 44–45; Lennox McLendon/AP Images, 47; Sven Simon/Imago/Icon SMI, 48; Red McLendon/AP Images, 51; Anja Niedringhaus/AP Images, 52–53; Panoramic/zuma/Icon SMI, 57; David J. Phillip/AP Images, 58

Editor: Chrös McDougall
Series Designer: Craig Hinton

Library of Congress Control Number: 2014932869

Cataloging-in-Publication Data
Rosen, Karen.
 Great moments in Olympic track & field / Karen Rosen.
   p. cm. -- (Great moments in Olympic sports)
Includes bibliographical references and index.
ISBN 978-1-62403-400-8
1. Track and field--Juvenile literature. 2. Olympics--Juvenile literature. I. Title.
796.42--dc23

                                                                    2014932869

796.42
ROS

Contents

Introduction

Track and field was the first Olympic sport. The ancient Olympic Games began with a footrace. The best athletes ran for glory in Olympia, Greece, nearly 2,800 years ago. Only men could compete. Other events were added over time.

The modern Olympic Games began in 1896 in Athens, Greece. Running, jumping, and throwing were still an important part of the Games. And still, only men were allowed. The first track events were the 100, 400, 800, 1,500, and 110-meter hurdles, as well as the marathon. The first field events were the discus, shot put, high jump, long jump, triple jump, and pole vault.

Women first participated in the 1900 Olympics. However, they were barred from Olympic track and field until 1928. Their first events were the 100 and 800 meters, plus the 4x100-meter relay, high jump, and discus. Some women looked worn out after the first 800-meter final that year. Olympic officials refused to hold that race again until 1960. By 1984, however, women were running the marathon.

Today, men compete in 24 events. Women have 23 events. The difference is the men also have a 50-kilometer walk.

Tracks, equipment, shoes, and timing systems have improved a lot since 1896. So have the athletes, who live up to the Olympic motto: Faster, Higher, Stronger.

Berlin 1936
A SYMBOL OF STRENGTH

Jesse Owens was the right man at the right time in history. The 1936 Olympic Games were in Berlin, Germany. Adolf Hitler was in power in Germany. His Nazi party believed in a "master race." Their propaganda said "Aryan" people with white skin, blond hair, and blue eyes were superior to other races.

Owens and other black American athletes helped show that theory was wrong. He had become a world-class sprinter and long jumper at Ohio State University. Then he proved his abilities by winning four gold medals at the

Jesse Owens became an Olympic legend for thriving in the face of adversity at the 1936 Olympic Games in Berlin, Germany.

1936 Olympics. But Owens got help in winning one of his gold medals.
The help came from a German athlete with blond hair and blue eyes.

An Unlikely Friend

Owens won his first gold medal in the 100-meter dash. As it turned out,
the German crowd loved him. They shouted "Jes-seeee O-wens" when he
was on the track. Owens then broke the Olympic record in the preliminary
heats of the 200 meters. On the same day, he also competed in the long
jump. He was a huge favorite. Owens had set a world record in the event
one year earlier at the Big Ten Championship meet. His performance that
day in Michigan was one of the greatest in sports history. Owens broke
three world records and equaled a fourth in the span of 45 minutes. His
long jump record of 26 feet, 8.25 inches (8.13 m) would last for 25 years.

Michael Johnson

Sprinters often "double" by running the 100 meters and 200 meters.
Michael Johnson of the United States decided to try something much
harder. He wanted to be the first man to win the 200 and 400 at the same
Olympics. Johnson had special gold shoes made for the occasion. At the
1996 Olympics in Atlanta, Georgia, he ran the 400 in 43.49 seconds. He won
by the largest margin of victory in that race in 100 years. In the 200, Johnson
set a new world record of 19.32 seconds.

8

German long jumper Luz Long, *left*, chats with Jesse Owens between jumps at the 1936 Olympics.

But the long jump in Berlin started out badly. Owens did not know that practice runs were not allowed. He ran through the pit in his sweats. Officials counted that as his first attempt. Owens was stunned.

He then fouled his second attempt. Owens had to reach the qualifying mark of 23 feet, 5.5 inches (7.15 m) on his third attempt. If he didn't, he would be out. He couldn't afford another foul.

That's when the German champion approached Owens. The American had met Luz Long in the Olympic Village. Long's career best was a foot shorter than Owens's best. But the German wanted to help. He told Owens that he should be able to qualify with his eyes closed.

Owens recalled Long's advice: "Jesse, let me make a suggestion. I will place my towel a foot in front of the foul line and you can use this for your takeoff. You should then qualify easily." On his final try, Owens took off a foot and a half before the board. This time, he easily qualified for the final round.

The final was later that afternoon. Owens had regained his confidence. His first jump was 25-4.75 (7.74 m), a new Olympic record. He then improved to 25-10 (7.87 m). On the fifth of six jumps, Long equaled that distance. Owens came back with a leap of 26-0.75 (7.94 m). He then hit 26-5.5 (8.06 m). That was an Olympic record that stood until 1960.

Carl Lewis

Carl Lewis was a young boy when he met Jesse Owens. Owens challenged the young athlete to work hard. At the 1984 Olympics in Los Angeles, California, Lewis won four gold medals. They were the same four events Owens won in 1936. Owens's granddaughter had carried the Olympic flame at the 1984 Opening Ceremony. "I just felt that Jesse was there in spirit," Lewis said. Owens competed in just one Olympics. Lewis appeared in four. He was the first athlete to win the long jump four times. Lewis also was the first man to win the 100 meters twice. He originally won the silver in 1988, but Canadian Ben Johnson was disqualified for doping.

Long was the first to congratulate him. Long put his arm around Owens, and they walked together down the runway. They were right in front of the box where German chancellor Hitler sat.

"It took a lot of courage for him to befriend me in front of Hitler," Owens later wrote. "You can melt down all the medals and cups I have, and they wouldn't be a plating on the 24-karat friendship I felt for Luz Long at that moment. Hitler must have gone crazy watching us embrace."

A Lasting Legacy

There is a myth that Hitler refused to greet Owens. They never did meet. But Hitler actually snubbed another black US athlete named Cornelius Johnson. Hitler had congratulated winners from Germany and Finland in his box. But he left the stadium once Johnson won the high jump. The International Olympic Committee (IOC) told Hitler he could greet everyone or no one. He chose no one. "Let it be said that we lost no sleep over not being greeted by Adolf Hitler," Owens said.

Owens went on to win the 200 meters in an Olympic-record time of 20.7 seconds. Mack Robinson won the silver medal. Robinson's younger brother Jackie later broke the color barrier in Major League Baseball in 1947. Owens also was part of the winning 4x100-meter relay team.

Jesse Owens, *center*, stands atop the medal podium after winning the long jump at the 1936 Olympics as silver medalist Luz Long of Germany, *right*, performs the Nazi salute.

Owens never saw Long again. Long was killed fighting for the Germans in 1943 during World War II. However, Owens met Long's son during the making of a 1960s documentary called *Jesse Owens Returns to Berlin*. They posed just like Owens and Long did in 1936. Owens said Long was a special athlete who "showed a special grace and a special courtesy when I needed help."

Athens 1896
AN OLYMPIC FIRST

James Connolly was a student at Harvard University when he read that the ancient competition known as the Olympic Games was being revived. Athletes from around the world were invited. The first of the modern Olympic Games would be held in 1896 in Athens, Greece. That was near where the ancient Olympics were held centuries earlier. The Olympics were largely unknown to most people at the time.

James Connolly poses with an American flag at Panathenaic Stadium at the 1896 Olympic Games in Athens, Greece.

Officials at Harvard didn't deem the event worthy of an excused absence. So the 27-year-old American left college in search of adventure.

Connolly and nine teammates traveled 16 days on a ship to Naples, Italy. When they arrived, someone stole Connolly's wallet. He reported it to the police. In his autobiography, Connolly remembered the police tried to keep him for questioning. But Connolly had no time to spare. He bolted free and ran for his train, which was pulling out of the station. It was a good thing Connolly had spring in his legs, because he had to leap for it.

"Three good pals . . . grabbed me so I wouldn't fall back overboard and hauled me through the compartment window," Connolly wrote. "I did not know it then, but if I had missed that train I would not have reached Athens in time for my event in the Games."

A Wild Journey

The US team arrived in Athens on the night of April 5, 1896. The next morning, they awoke to the sound of a brass band. What was going on? The athletes thought they had 12 days until the Olympics started. They found out they were using the wrong calendar. The Greeks back then used the Julian calendar. The United States used the Gregorian calendar, which most people still use today. The US athletes had to spring into action. The Olympics were beginning that very day.

Inside the marble Panathenaic Stadium, Connolly discovered that the triple jump runway was soft. He said his heel sank 2 inches (5 cm) with every stride. The triple jump is often called the hop, step, and jump. The rules at the time also allowed two hops and a jump. So Connolly decided to use two hops and a jump for the first time since he was a boy.

He needed only two attempts. Officials were not supposed to tell athletes how far they had jumped. But when Connolly complained, the man raking the pit told him he was so far ahead and he might as well go back to the dressing room and take his bath. Connolly had gone 44 feet, 11.75 inches (13.71 m). He beat his nearest competitor by more than 3 feet (0.91 m).

The First Marathon

The Greeks needed a hero at the 1896 Olympic Games. The marathon was the last chance for the host country to win a track-and-field gold medal. This race was even more special because of its history. According to legend, in 490 BCE, a messenger ran from the Battle of Marathon to Athens. He said, "Victory!" and dropped dead. Luckily, nobody died at the 1896 Olympics. The Greeks, though, got their champion. He was Spiridon Louis, who ran the nearly 25 miles in shoes donated by his village. In the stadium, two Greek princes ran onto the track to escort Louis to the finish line. The marathon was later extended to the current 26.2 miles at the 1908 Olympics.

As the crowd cheered, Connolly began pulling on his pants. "The 80,000 spectators in the seats were rising," he wrote. "I then came alive and stood to attention. The 200-piece band had broken into the 'Star-Spangled Banner.'" As he saw an American flag raised, Connolly realized that the national anthem was playing in his honor.

Connolly's first thought, he later recalled: "You're the first Olympic victor in 1,500 years." Then he thought to himself, "The gang back home will be tickled when they hear of it!"

The last Olympic champion before Connolly was boxer Prince Varasdates of Armenia in the year 369. Connolly wasn't finished, though. He also placed second in the high jump and third in the long jump.

Dorando Pietri

Spectators at the 1908 Olympic Games in London, England, knew there was a problem as soon as they saw Dorando Pietri. When he came into the Olympic Stadium for the last lap of the marathon, he went the wrong way. The little Italian man was so worn out he would collapse five times. Officials kept picking him up. They also helped him stagger across the finish line first. The American team, urged by athlete-turned-journalist James Connolly, protested that US runner Johnny Hayes was the real winner because Pietri had help. Pietri was disqualified and "lay between life and death," said the official report. He got better, however, and became such a huge celebrity that songs were written about him.

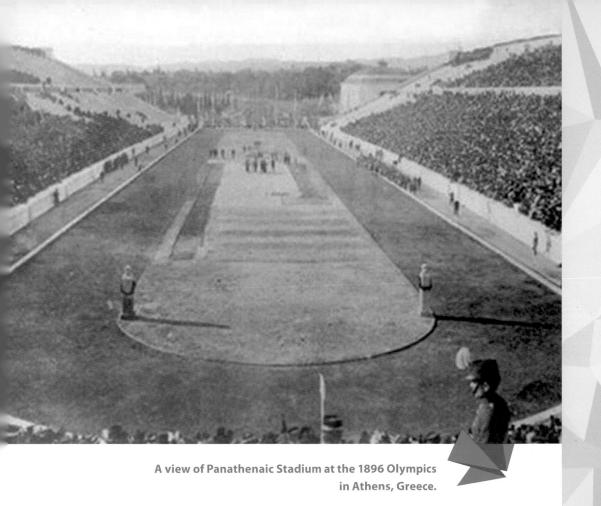

A view of Panathenaic Stadium at the 1896 Olympics
in Athens, Greece.

Connolly later wrote many books, including one called *An Olympic Victor*, which featured the story of Spiridon Louis. While Connolly will forever be the first Olympic champion, it would be wrong to call him a gold medalist. At the 1896 Olympics, there were no gold medals. The winner received a silver medal. The runner-up was given a bronze medal. The third-place finisher didn't get any medal at all.

Stockholm 1912
THE GREATEST ATHLETE

Athletes in the decathlon don't have to be good at just one event. They have to be good at 10 of them. They have to sprint. They have to hurdle. They have to jump and throw. To top it off, they have to run nearly a mile. The event became one of glamour and prestige. The Olympic decathlon champions would be among the most revered athletes of their time. That tradition started with Jim Thorpe's historic performance at the 1912 Olympic Games in Stockholm, Sweden.

Jim Thorpe poses in his Team USA clothes at the 1912 Olympic Games in Stockholm, Sweden.

Thorpe's story began in Oklahoma. He was born into the Sac and Fox tribe. He was given the name Wa-Tho-Huck, meaning Bright Path.

Thorpe's path was brightest in athletics. He played college football for Carlisle Indian School in Pennsylvania. He was a two-time All-American. Thorpe earned varsity letters in 11 different sports. He was so good on his feet that he was also the college ballroom dancing champion in 1912.

At the 1912 Olympics, Thorpe started out by winning the pentathlon. The track-and-field pentathlon is no longer an Olympic event. Similar to the decathlon, the pentathlon is a combination of five events. In Stockholm, Thorpe won four of them. They were the 200-meter dash, 1,500-meter run, discus, and long jump. In the other event, javelin, he was third. That was despite only having practiced the javelin for two months. Needless to say, Thorpe easily won the gold medal.

The Flying Finns

"The Flying Finns" were a group of runners from Finland in the 1920s and 1930s. The greatest was Paavo Nurmi, who usually carried a stopwatch to check his pace. On one day at the 1924 Olympics in Paris, France, he pulled off an amazing double. First, Nurmi easily won the 1,500 meters. Then, he came back approximately one hour later to run in the 5,000 meters. With a little more than a lap to go, Nurmi threw his stopwatch in the grass. He held off teammate Ville Ritola for another gold medal. From 1920 to 1928, Nurmi won 12 Olympic medals. Nine of those medals were gold.

The next day, Thorpe tied for fourth in the Olympic high jump. Four days after that, he was seventh in the long jump. Then it was time for Thorpe to try his first decathlon. The grueling, two-day event is considered one of the greatest challenges in sports. Thorpe took to it with ease.

He won the shot put, high jump, 110-meter hurdles, and 1,500 meters. He also did well in the other events: the long jump, 100 meters, 400 meters, pole vault, discus, and javelin. In decathlon, each result is awarded points based on a scoring table. Thorpe's total was an incredible 8,412 points. That was 688 points better than the runner-up, Hugo Wieslander of Sweden. It was also almost 1,000 points more than the old world record of 7,414.

After Thorpe won the decathlon, the King of Sweden gave him an award. He said, "Sir, you are the greatest athlete in the world." Thorpe replied, "Thanks, King."

Hard Times to Come

Thorpe came home to a parade down Broadway in New York. The Native American athlete received a hero's welcome. "I heard people yelling my name," he said later, "and I couldn't realize how one fellow could have so many friends."

But Thorpe's world fell apart in early 1913. A story came out that he had accepted $25 per week to play minor league baseball in North Carolina in 1909 and 1910. The rules at that time said Olympic athletes had to be amateurs. By taking money, Thorpe was considered a professional. That meant he should not have been allowed into the Olympics. Thorpe's medals were taken away from him. His name was removed from the record books.

He went on to play pro baseball and football. But times were hard. Thorpe was a construction worker. He took small roles in movies. He also worked other odd jobs. As an athlete, however, Thorpe was not forgotten. In fact, the Associated Press voted Thorpe as the greatest athlete of the first half of the 1900s.

Jackie Joyner-Kersee

Jackie Joyner-Kersee was named after Jackie Kennedy, then the first lady of the United States. Her grandmother said, "Someday this girl will be the first lady of something." "JJK" was one of the world's best multievent athletes by the time she competed in the 1984 Olympics in Los Angeles, California. But she ran poorly in the 800 meters, the seventh and final event of the heptathlon. She lost the gold medal by just five points. Four years later in Seoul, South Korea, Joyner-Kersee hurt her left knee early in the competition. That couldn't stop her. She ran her second-fastest time ever in the 800. Her final score was 7,291 points. She had smashed her own world record by 76 points.

Jim Thorpe competes in the long jump at the 1912 Olympics.

Thorpe never gave up trying to reclaim his Olympic achievements. His appeals began in 1914. They were still unsuccessful when he died in 1953. Finally, in 1982, the IOC changed its ruling. Thorpe was again an Olympic champion. His children were given his medals a few months later. Today, many Olympic competitors are professionals and make money from their sports.

London 1948
THE FLYING HOUSEWIFE

Fanny Blankers-Koen was nicknamed "The Flying Housewife." Some people during her time thought she should be a stay-at-home housewife.

The Dutch athlete competed in her first Olympics in 1936 in Berlin, Germany. She was then 18 years old. Blankers-Koen was sixth in the high jump and fifth as a member of the Dutch team in the 4x100-meter relay. The highlight of the Games for her was getting Jesse Owens's autograph.

Dutch athlete Fanny Blankers-Koen leaps over the final hurdle in the 80-meter race at the 1948 Olympic Games in London, England.

Because of World War II, the Olympics were not held again until 1948. By that time, Blankers-Koen was 30 years old. She had married her coach and they had two young children. But Blankers-Koen was still an athlete. She held six world records. Four of those records were in individual events. When she said she planned to compete at the 1948 Olympics in London, England, however, some people thought that was inappropriate for a woman like her.

A British Olympic official said, "Why is a 30-year-old mother of two running in short pants at the expense of leaving her family?"

Blankers-Koen replied, "I will show him."

She sure did.

Running Away with Gold

The rules at that time allowed women to enter only three individual events. Blankers-Koen chose the 100 meters, 200 meters, and 80-meter hurdles. That meant she could not compete in the high jump and long jump even though she was the world-record holder. However, she was allowed to race on the Dutch relay team.

Blankers-Koen's first event was the 100. She won easily on a muddy track. The headline in one London paper said, "Fastest Woman in the World Is an Expert Cook."

Her next race was the hurdles. This race was not so easy. Blankers-Koen hit a hurdle. At the finish line, she leaned so low the tape cut her neck. Blankers-Koen was not sure she'd won. Then the band started playing "God Save the King." It was the British national anthem. Blankers-Koen thought that indicated Maureen Gardner of Great Britain was the winner. Then Blankers-Koen found out why the anthem was playing. It was announcing the arrival of King George VI. Soon after, she was declared the winner by one foot.

"See, you aren't too old after all," her husband told her.

But Blankers-Koen was not happy. She was crying in the stadium dressing rooms before her next event, the 200 meters. "Even though I had won the two gold medals, I was very depressed," she said later. "The press

Babe Didrikson

Babe Didrikson had many talents. She won six events at the 1932 US Olympic Trials. In those days, women could enter just three individual Olympic events. At the Olympics in Los Angeles, California, Didrikson won the javelin. Then she broke the world record in the 80-meter hurdles. In the high jump, Didrikson and Jean Shiley both cleared a world-record height. The judges ruled that Didrikson's jump was illegal in the jump-off. So she shared the world record but was given second place. Didrikson also excelled in swimming, basketball, baseball, and golf. She also could type 86 words a minute, won a blue ribbon for sewing, and could play the harmonica.

would not stop questioning me, and I got even sadder after talking to my children in Amsterdam who said they missed me. So I told my husband I would not compete anymore and would go home."

Her husband, Jan, told her that if she stayed, she could win four gold medals. She would be just like her idol Jesse Owens. "OK, I'll stay," Blankers-Koen said. "I'll call the children and tell them they must wait."

She won the 200-meter final by the widest margin of victory in Olympic history. Her final event was the 4x100 relay. Blankers-Koen ran the anchor leg. She got the baton in fourth place. Then she passed the other runners to win her fourth gold medal. As one newspaper said, "Holland has won four gold medals in Olympic track and field history . . . and Fanny has won them all."

Harrison Dillard

It wasn't a surprise that Harrison Dillard won a gold medal at the 1948 Olympics. But few could have predicted that he'd win the 100-meter dash. Dillard was called "Bones" because he'd been such a skinny boy. He was the world-record holder in the 110-meter hurdles. At the US Olympic Trials, he hit some hurdles. He did not finish the race. Luckily, Dillard already had made the Olympic team in the 100 meters. At the 1948 Games in London, England, he beat the favorites for the gold medal. Dillard also competed at the 1952 Olympics in Helsinki, Finland. This time, he ran in his first love, the 110-meter hurdles. Dillard won another gold medal.

Fanny Blankers-Koen of the Netherlands, *right*, crosses the finish line first in the 100-meter final at the 1948 Olympic Games.

If she were competing today, Blankers-Koen could enter as many events as she qualified for. Many people believe she could have won six gold medals in London if she had competed in the long jump and the high jump. The winning long jump was 22 inches (0.56 m) shorter than her world record. The winning high jump was 5 feet 6.25 (1.68 m). Blankers-Koen's world record was 5–7.25 (1.71 m).

When she returned home, there was a parade in her honor. Blankers-Koen rode through the streets of Amsterdam in a horse-drawn carriage with her husband and children. Her neighbors gave her a bicycle so she could "go through life at a slower pace." The British official who had criticized her wrote an apology. She happily accepted.

Rome 1960
AN ETERNAL PERFORMANCE

Wilma Rudolph was a sickly child. She almost died from scarlet fever and double pneumonia. Rudolph also had the measles and whooping cough. When she was four, she contracted polio, a terrible disease that can be crippling or even deadly. Rudolph had to wear a steel brace on her left leg until she was nine.

"My doctor told me I would never walk again," she wrote in her autobiography. "My mother told me I would. I believed my mother."

Wilma Rudolph overcame childhood polio to become one of the stars of the 1960 Olympic Games in Rome, Italy.

Rudolph's mother taught her many brothers and sisters how to help Rudolph with daily massages. "If it wasn't for my family, I probably would never have been able to walk properly, no less run," she wrote.

After Rudolph was well enough to take off the brace, she wore a special shoe. Then she didn't need the shoe any more. By age 12, Rudolph was "challenging every boy in our neighborhood at running, jumping, everything." She played basketball and ran track. At age 16, just five years after she had started running, Rudolph made the 1956 US Olympic team. She won a bronze medal on the 4x100-meter relay at the Games in Melbourne, Australia.

When Rudolph got home, she took the medal with her to school. It was passed around so much that it got handprints on it. Rudolph tried to shine it up. But, she said, "I discovered that bronze doesn't shine. So I decided I'm going to try this one more time. I'm going to go for the gold."

Chasing Gold

As a high school senior, Rudolph got pregnant and had a daughter. Tennessee State University coach Ed Temple did not allow mothers on his track team. But he made an exception for Rudolph. She became a Tennessee State Tigerbelle.

Rudolph continued her development. She was easily one of the world's best sprinters. Expectations for her were high going into the 1960 Olympics in Rome, Italy. But Rudolph's father decided he did not want her to go. He thought she should stay home with her daughter. Rudolph had the support of her mother, Blanche, and coach Temple, however. So she decided to go to the Olympics.

Rudolph ran into some bad luck in Rome. The day before her first 100-meter heat, she was jogging across the practice field and sprained her ankle. She iced it and wore tape to protect her ankle. The tape gave her extra stability as she got through her first heat and quarterfinal. In the semifinal, Rudolph equaled the world record of 11.30 seconds. Then she won the gold medal with a time of 11.0 seconds. That would have been a world record if it had not been wind-aided. The crowd in the

Abebe Bikila

Abebe Bikila's old running shoes were worn out. His new ones pinched his feet. He was afraid of blisters. That's why Bikila ran the 1960 Olympic marathon barefoot. The marathon was held at night on Roman streets lit by torches. Bikila, one of the Ethiopian emperor's bodyguards, made his move at a symbolic place. Bikila was passing the Obelisk of Axum, a monument Italy had stolen from Ethiopia in the buildup to World War II, when he pulled away. Bikila was the first man to win two straight Olympic marathons. He won in Tokyo, Japan, four years later. This time he was wearing shoes.

Stadio Olimpico chanted "Vilma! Vilma!" as she ran a victory lap. Italian newspapers called Rudolph "The Black Gazelle."

In the first heat of the 200, Rudolph set an Olympic record of 23.2 seconds. That was still shy of her world record of 22.9 seconds. In the final, she ran a slow time by her standards: 24.0 seconds. But she won by such a large amount that she was the only runner the camera caught in the photo finish.

"I always had the worst start in the history of any sprinter because of my size, and I was the tallest sprinter that had come from the US," said Rudolph, who was 5 feet 11. "My first 30–40 yards I was never in the race. The farther I ran the faster I became and I could always accelerate at the end. That was the key."

Flo Jo

Florence Griffith Joyner ran with style. She had long, colorful fingernails. She wore makeup when she competed. Sometimes she even wore flashy bodysuits. "Flo Jo" ran the 100 meters in 10.49 seconds at the 1988 US Olympic Trials. That made her the fastest woman in history. At the Olympics later that year in Seoul, South Korea, Griffith Joyner got so far ahead in the 100 that she started to smile. In the 200, Griffith Joyner clocked 21.34 seconds. She shattered her own world record. Though her marks made some people suspect doping, Griffith Joyner never failed a drug test. She died in 1998 when she was only 38 years old, but her records stood through 2013.

The 1960 US 4x100 relay team members, *from left*, Wilma Rudolph, Barbara Jones, Lucinda Williams, and Martha Hudson, pose with their gold medals.

The four members of the US 4x100 relay team were all Tennessee State Tigerbelles. They set a world record of 44.4 seconds in the semifinals. In the final, Rudolph fumbled the exchange from Lucinda Williams. She did not drop the baton, though. She regained the lead to beat Germany with a time of 44.5 seconds. Rudolph said later that the relay was the victory that was most important to her.

"For then I could stand on the podium with my Tigerbelle teammates whom I love," she said, "and we could celebrate together."

6

Mexico City 1968
BEAMONESQUE

On the first moonwalk in 1969, Neil Armstrong said, "That's one small step for man, one giant leap for mankind." Nine months earlier, Bob Beamon had taken a giant leap on earth.

The American was the favorite in the long jump at the 1968 Olympic Games in Mexico City, Mexico. That year, Beamon had won 22 of 23 meets he entered. In one contest, he jumped a personal best 27 feet, 6.5 inches (8.39 m). It would have been a world record. However, it was wind-aided so it did not count.

US long jumper Bob Beamon shattered the world record at the 1968 Olympics in Mexico City, Mexico.

Beamon almost did not get a chance to show what he could do at the Olympics. In the preliminaries, he fouled on his first two jumps. If he took off past the board on his third jump, he would be out. US teammate Ralph Boston stepped in to help. Boston was the Olympic gold medalist in 1960 and won the silver in 1964. He also was the co-holder of the world record of 27-4.75 (8.35 m).

Boston told Beamon to make a mark a few inches before the board. It was the same kind of help German Luz Long gave Jesse Owens in 1936. Beamon took off with room to spare and qualified for the final.

On the day of the final, the first three jumpers fouled. Beamon was next. Boston said to him, "Come on, make it a good one." He sure did. Beamon took off and sailed high into the air. He was able to maintain the height and landed in the sand perfectly. Beamon's jump was so long that

Al Oerter

In four straight Olympic discus competitions, Al Oerter was never the favorite. Yet he won four straight gold medals. The first came at the 1956 Olympics in Melbourne, Australia. Oerter was just 20 years old. The next year, he almost died in a car accident. Oerter recovered and won in 1960 in Rome, Italy. He was injured and wearing a neck brace when he arrived in Tokyo, Japan, for the 1964 Olympics. Oerter hurt himself even more on a fall in practice. He still won. Finally, at the 1968 Olympics in Mexico City, Mexico, Oerter threw 5 feet (1.52 m) farther than his personal best.

the measuring device slid off its rail before reaching the mark. Officials had to use an old fashioned steel tape.

Finally, they announced that the jump was 8.90 meters. Beamon knew he had jumped far, but he didn't know how far. He did not know the conversion of the distance into feet and inches. Then Boston told him. Beamon had jumped 29 feet, 2.5 inches. No one in history had even jumped 28 feet. Beamon had added 1 foot, 9.75 Inches (55 cm) to the world record with one amazing leap.

Realizing the enormity of what he had done, Beamon was overcome with emotion. He crumpled to his knees and had to be helped to his feet. Lynn Davies, the defending champion from Great Britain, was not sure he even wanted to compete.

"What's the point?" he said. "He's destroyed the event."

Rain began to fall, which also hurt the chances of the other long jumpers. Beamon took only one more jump. He went 26-4.5 (8.04 m) and passed on his other four attempts. He knew the gold medal was his.

"It was an incredible surprise," Beamon said. "As a matter of fact we never thought the record would pass 27 feet 10, or 8.4 meters, but I like surprises."

The silver medalist, Klaus Beer of East Germany, also had the best jump of his life. He only improved by four inches to go 26-10.5 (8.19 m). Boston won the bronze medal. His longest jump was 26-9.25 (8.16 m).

Beamon's jump inspired a new word. "Beamonesque" means an incredible athletic performance. Beamon was so amazed by his performance that he couldn't duplicate it. He never even got close. His best after that memorable day was 26-11.5 (8.21 m).

Utterly Dominant

Some people said Beamon had been helped by the high altitude in Mexico City. It is 7,943 feet (2,421 m) above sea level. There is less air resistance at altitude. However, every athlete had the same conditions.

Jim Ryun

Going into the 1968 Olympics, American Jim Ryun was unbeaten at 1,500 meters ("the metric mile") for three years. But he was not at his best in Mexico City, Mexico. Ryun wasn't used to the high altitude. He'd also had mononucleosis four months before the Games. Meanwhile, his main rival, Kip Keino, trained at altitude in Kenya. Keino was already the silver medalist in the 5,000. But he had problems, too. He was in pain from an infected gallbladder. In addition, bad traffic on the way to the stadium forced him to jog the last mile. It didn't seem to matter. Keino's strategy was to build a big lead. Although Ryun was known for his finishing kick, he couldn't catch Keino and settled for silver.

Bob Beamon flies through the air on his record-breaking long jump at the 1968 Olympics.

Other people said that the wind reading on Beamon's jump was suspicious. It was exactly 2.0 meters (6-6.75 feet) per second. If it had been any stronger, the jump would not have been a legal record. The doubts bothered Beamon. "Some people said I made a lucky jump in the Olympics," he said. "After a while, that kind of talk gets into your mind."

Beamon's record stood for 23 years. US jumper Mike Powell finally broke it. He jumped 29-4.5 (8.95 m) not at altitude at the 1991 World Championships in Tokyo, Japan. The World Championships is the biggest track meet in non-Olympic years.

Los Angeles 1984
BREAKING THROUGH

I t's normal today to see women competing in road races or running to stay in shape. Until 1984, however, the longest Olympic women's running event was 1,500 meters. That's less than a mile. Two women's track events were added at the 1984 Olympic Games in Los Angeles, California. They were the 3,000 meters and, more important, the marathon.

Men had been running the marathon since the first modern Olympics in 1896. Since 1921, the race had been 26.2 miles long. Pioneering women had shown

American Joan Benoit runs in the marathon at the 1984 Olympic Games in Los Angeles, California.

that females could run that distance, too. One of those women was Joan Benoit. The American ran a time of 2 hours, 22 minutes, 43 seconds at the 1983 Boston Marathon. That was faster than any other woman in history by two minutes. She was ready to make her mark in the Olympics.

Benoit injured her right knee training for the US Olympic Marathon Trials. She was in so much pain she could barely walk. Benoit had to have surgery. Just 17 days later, Benoit won the Trials. Now she was truly ready.

Leading the Pack

Fifty women from 28 countries started the 1984 Olympic marathon. Some of the women were better at 5,000 meters or 10,000 meters. But those races were not in the Olympics at that time. Benoit, however, was a

Billy Mills

It has been called the greatest upset in Olympic history. When Billy Mills won the 10,000 meters at the 1964 Olympics in Tokyo, Japan, one of the officials asked him, "Who are you?" Mills, an Oglala Sioux Native American, was a surprise challenger. World-record holder Ron Clarke of Australia was the favorite. Mohamed Gammoudi of Tunisia also came into Tokyo as an underdog. Yet the trio was so fast they lapped other runners. The slower runners were in their way. Clarke shoved Mills to get through, then Gammoudi pushed between them. Mills wove through the lapped runners. He passed Clarke and Gammoudi, winning the gold medal on sheer determination.

The women who ran the 1984 Olympic marathon proved that women were capable of endurance running.

marathon star. That showed just 14 minutes into the race. Thinking that the pace was too slow, she moved into the lead.

"I did not want to take the lead," she said, "but I promised myself I'd run my race and nobody else's and that's exactly what I did."

Benoit skipped the first water stop to stay ahead of the pack. Other runners thought Benoit would not be able to keep up her pace. They thought the heat would affect her. They thought they would eventually catch her. They were wrong. Wearing a white painter's cap to shield her from the sun, Benoit ran alone. She led by 13 seconds at 5 miles (8.0 km). At 19 miles (30.6 km), she had a comfortable two-minute cushion.

Joan Benoit runs uncontested through the Los Angeles Coliseum toward the finish line at the 1984 Olympic marathon.

No spectators were allowed on a 3-mile (4.8-km) stretch of the Marina Freeway. "The one thing I'll tell my grandchildren," Benoit said later, "is that one time I ran alone on an LA freeway." The race ended in the main Olympic stadium. As Benoit got closer, she passed a giant mural of herself winning in Boston. She was a little embarrassed, but also inspired.

Marathon runners entered the stadium through a tunnel. Benoit was a very private person. She knew she was about to be really famous. "Once you leave this tunnel," Benoit thought, "your life will be changed forever."

There were 77,000 cheering fans in the Los Angeles Coliseum. "You're not finished," she told herself, "Get around the track and nail this thing down." With half a lap to go, she waved her hat at the crowd and smiled. Her winning time was 2:24:52.

Building upon a Movement

Footraces have always been in the Olympics. Casual running in the United States took off after the 1972 Olympics. American Frank Shorter won the marathon at those Olympic Games in Munich, West Germany. Soon many more people were running. The running movement grew even more after Benoit's win, particularly among women.

"My high school didn't have a girls' track team when I started running," she said later. "I'm just happy that I could be part of the women's running revolution, and the boom. I think women make good runners because they're so good at multitasking, and it's something they can fit into their

Emil Zatopek

Emil Zatopek did not look like he was having fun when he ran. He would pant and wheeze and make a face like he was in pain. "This isn't gymnastics or ice skating, you know," he said. The 1952 Olympics were held in Helsinki, Finland. There, the Czech runner did something no one else has done. He won the 10,000 meters easily. Four days later, Zatopek won the 5,000. Then he entered the marathon. It didn't matter that Zatopek had never run one before. He won by more than two-and-a-half minutes. Zatopek wasn't the only gold medalist in his family. His wife Dana won the javelin.

busy schedules. Running is more accessible and affordable than a lot of other sports and fitness activities. It can also be very social, which draws women in."

About 15 minutes after Benoit's victory, another runner entered the stadium in shocking condition. Gabriela Andersen-Schiess of Switzerland staggered onto the track. Her body looked twisted. But she refused help. If anyone touched her, she would be disqualified like Dorando Pietri in 1908. It took Andersen-Schiess almost six minutes to complete her lap. She stopped sometimes, but then kept going. Finally, Andersen-Schiess collapsed across the finish line. Then the medics could touch her. Andersen-Schiess placed thirty-seventh. With her time of 2:48:42, she would have won the first five Olympic men's marathons.

Andersen-Schiess recovered quickly. People admired her determination to finish. Her name became famous, too. It was a great change from the first Olympic women's track competition. In 1928, women looked so tired after the 800 meters that the race was not held again until 1960. The women's marathon did not have to worry about being canceled. However, now there is a rule called the "Schiess" rule. It says medics can touch athletes to see if they are OK without the athlete being disqualified.

Beijing 2008
LIGHTNING BOLT

The Olympic gold medalist in the 100-meter dash earns the honorary title "The Fastest Man in the World." That was not enough for Usain Bolt of Jamaica. He made it his goal to become a legend. And that is what he did at the 2008 Olympic Games in Beijing, China. Bolt's performances in the 100, 200, and 4x100-meter relay were world-record fast. He won his first race despite easing up at the finish. And he did it with his left shoe untied. Even Bolt's name sounds fast.

Jamaican sprinter Usain Bolt celebrates as he crosses the 100-meter finish line in world-record time at the 2008 Olympic Games in Beijing, China.

He strikes a "lightning pose" after he wins races. Bolt calls the pose "To the World."

When he was young, Bolt originally liked a sport called cricket. He wasn't very good at it. Track and field suited him better. That's because Bolt was 6 feet 4 by the time he was 15 years old. He then grew one more inch. Bolt has a very long stride. He also has a fast turnover. That means Bolt can get his feet to the ground more times than other sprinters.

Bolt's main race was originally the 200 meters. He wanted to run the 100, but his coach would not let him. They made a deal. If Bolt broke the national record in the 200, he could run the 100. Bolt broke that record in 2007. It had been standing for 36 years. Now he could run the 100. In only his fourth 100 as a professional athlete, Bolt broke the world record. He ran 9.72 seconds. His rival, Tyson Gay of the United States, was second in 9.85.

Showdown in China

People expected Gay and Asafa Powell to be Bolt's top rivals at the 2008 Olympics. Powell, who is also from Jamaica, defeated Bolt by one-hundredth of a second a month before the Games. Bolt knew he would need to be at his best to win an Olympic gold medal. He wanted to make sure he did not feel sick on race day. So he followed a special diet while he was in China. In his autobiography, *Faster Than Lightning*, Bolt wrote that he ate 100 chicken nuggets a day, 20 at a time. "When you eat what you know, your stomach won't get upset," he explained.

The 100-meter dash was Bolt's first event. When the gun went off, Bolt was the second slowest out of the blocks. Too many nuggets? But he took the lead by the halfway point. Soon he was running away from the competition. With about 15 meters to go, Bolt let up. He wanted to celebrate. He spread his arms and beat his chest as he crossed the finish line. Bolt's time was still amazing. He clocked 9.69 seconds, breaking his own world record easily.

The race was also the fastest in history. Six men had times faster than 10 seconds. Richard Thompson of Trinidad and Tobago was second.

An Emotional Finish

Derek Redmond eased through the first two rounds of the 400 meters at the 1992 Olympic Games in Barcelona, Spain. In his semifinal, though, he felt a pop. His hamstring had torn. The British sprinter collapsed onto the track in agony. He got up when he saw workers approaching him with a stretcher. Redmond started to limp and hop, determined to finish the race. "With 100 meters to go, I felt a hand on my shoulder," he said. "It was my old man." Redmond's father had come out of the stands. He held off officials who wanted the crying runner to quit. Father and son crossed the finish line together.

His time was 9.89 seconds. That was just .02 ahead of Walter Dix of Team USA. Powell was fifth. Gay did not even make the final.

People wondered how fast Bolt could have run if he had tried as hard as he could until the finish line. Scientists studied the question. They said he could have run 9.55 seconds. Critics thought Bolt should not have eased up for a different reason. IOC president Jacques Rogge said it was a "little disrespectful."

"I wasn't bragging," Bolt said. "When I thought I had the field covered I was celebrating. I was happy."

Next up for Bolt was the 200-meter finals. This time he did not ease up. He leaned at the finish line to get an even faster time. Bolt broke

Breaking the Streak

Bad luck used to follow the US women's 4x100-meter relay team at the Olympics. In 2004, Team USA was disqualified in the final for making a baton exchange outside the passing zone. Four years later, the US runners dropped the baton in the first round. At the 2012 London Olympics, Team USA made up for lost time. Tianna Madison got the US off to a fast start. She handed off to Allyson Felix, and then Bianca Knight ran the third leg. Carmelita Jeter came home in 40.82 seconds, smashing the 27-year-old world record. Felix and Knight weren't even born when East Germany set the old mark of 41.37 seconds. "It's a relief. It's a joy," Felix said. "We were confident in the passes, and it showed."

Jamaica's Usain Bolt obliterates the pack to win the 100-meter dash in world-record time at the 2008 Olympics.

American Michael Johnson's 12-year-old world record of 19.32 seconds. Bolt's time was 19.30. The next day was Bolt's twenty-second birthday. He then got his third gold medal and third world record. Bolt ran the third leg on the Jamaican 4x100-meter relay team.

Bolt showed his amazing performance was not just a flash in the pan. A year later, he ran 9.58 seconds in the 100 meters at the 2009 World Championships. He also won the 200 and the relay.

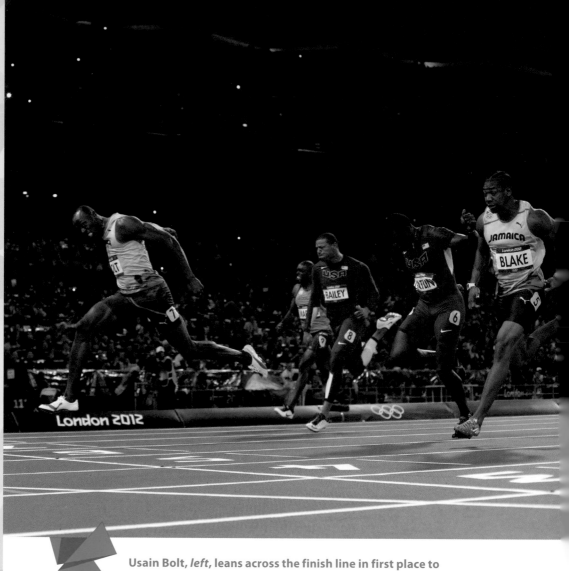

Usain Bolt, *left*, leans across the finish line in first place to defend his 100-meter gold medal at the 2012 Olympics.

Defending His Title

The 2012 Olympic Games were in London, England. Bolt was one of the biggest stars going into the Games. He talked about what he wanted to accomplish.

"I'm working as hard as possible so I can go as fast as possible," he said. "[The fans] want to see my personality, me enjoying it and doing crazy stuff, but they also want to see that [record-breaking] time. If I dominate the Olympics, I'll be a living legend. A living legend walking around. Sounds good."

Bolt indeed wowed fans in London. He won the 100 and 200, although not in world-record time. Still, after the 200, he bragged, "I am now a living legend. Bask in my glory." Bolt had one more event in London, the 4x100 relay. The Jamaicans set a world record.

Super Saturday

It has been called the greatest night in British track and field. Home fans at the 2012 Olympic Games in London, England, were eager for something to cheer about. The crowd at the Olympic Stadium went wild when Jessica Ennis won the heptathlon. Then Greg Rutherford added another gold medal for Great Britain in the long jump. Mo Farah capped it off by winning the 10,000 meters for his country's first victory in that race. In total, Team GB won six gold medals on that unforgettable Saturday. "If it hadn't been for the support of the crowd I don't think I'd have won that race," Farah said. "To win the Olympics in your own country is the greatest feeling in the world."

Great Olympians

Fanny Blankers-Koen (Netherlands)

The Dutch housewife with two children won four gold medals at the 1948 Olympics.

Usain Bolt (Jamaica)

The Jamaican sensation won three gold medals at both the 2008 and 2012 Olympics. In Beijing, Bolt set world records in all three events (100, 200, and 4x100).

Babe Didrikson (USA)

She won two gold medals (javelin, 80-meter hurdles) and a silver medal (high jump) at the 1932 Games.

Jackie Joyner-Kersee (USA)

She won six total medals, including gold in heptathlon (1988 and 1992) and long jump (1988) over four Olympics.

Carl Lewis (USA)

He ended his career in 1996 with nine gold medals and one silver. Lewis is the only athlete to win the long jump four straight times.

Paavo Nurmi (Finland)

From 1920 to 1928, the distance runner won a record nine gold and three silver medals. He won five gold medals in 1924.

Al Oerter (USA)

Oerter is the only athlete to win the discus in four straight Olympic Games: 1956, 1960, 1964, and 1968.

Jesse Owens (USA)

As a black athlete winning four gold medals (100, 200, long jump, and 4x100) at the 1936 Olympics, Owens disproved the Nazi theory of Aryan supremacy.

Wilma Rudolph (USA)

After winning a bronze medal in the 4x100 in 1956, Rudolph won the 100, 200, and 4x100 gold medals in 1960.

Emil Zatopek (Czechoslovakia)

In 1952, he became the only runner to win the 5,000, 10,000, and marathon in the same Olympics.

Glossary

AMATEUR
An athlete who cannot earn money for competing.

ANCHOR
The last of four runners on a relay team.

BATON
A short stick that each team member must carry while running a relay race.

CLEARED
To successfully make it over the bar in the high jump or pole vault.

DOPING
The use of illegal substances to get an unfair advantage.

FOUL
A violation, such as stepping over the board in long jump, that results in the athlete getting no mark for the attempt.

HEAT
One of multiple races in an event. In the Olympics, many races have preliminary heats to determine the fastest runners who make the finals.

KICK
A burst of speed at the end of a race.

LAPPED
When one runner goes a full lap ahead of a competitor.

PROPAGANDA
Misleading information put out to promote one's viewpoint.

WIND-AIDED
A result that counts in competition but is not eligible for the record books because the conditions were too windy.

For More
Information

SELECTED BIBLIOGRAPHY

Joyner-Kersee, Jackie, and Sonja Steptoe. *A Kind of Grace: The Autobiography of the World's Greatest Female Athlete.* New York: Grand Central Publishing, 1997.

Leder, Jane. *Grace & Glory: A Century of Women in the Olympics.* Chicago, IL: Triumph Books, 1996.

Wallechinsky, David, and Jaime Loucky. *The Complete Book of the Olympics: 2012 Edition.* London: Aurum Press, 2012.

FURTHER READINGS

Bolt, Usain. *Faster than Lightning: My Autobiography.* New York: HarperSport, 2013.

Farah, Mo. *Twin Ambitions – My Autobiography.* London: Hodder & Stoughton, 2013.

Johnson, Michael. *Gold Rush: What Makes an Olympic Champion?* New York: HarperSport, 2012.

WEBSITES

To learn more about Great Moments in Olympic Sports, visit **booklinks.abdopublishing.com**. These links are routinely monitored and updated to provide the most current information available.

PLACES TO VISIT

National Track & Field Hall of Fame
216 Fort Washington Ave.
New York, NY 10032
(212) 923-1803
www.armoryfoundation.org/what-we-do/hall-of-fame
This museum opened in 2004 in the historic Armory, which houses one of the fastest tracks in the world. Visitors can roam the exhibit space to learn about the rich history of track and field in the United States. The interactive displays teach students the importance of exercise, nutrition, teamwork, and dedication. The hall also features a miniature replica of the 26.2-mile New York City Marathon course.

US Olympic Training Center
1750 E Boulder St.
Colorado Springs, CO 80909
(719) 866-4618
www.teamusa.org
The US Olympic team has welcomed more than 1.6 million visitors to its headquarters in Colorado Springs, Colorado. In addition to extensive training facilities for elite athletes, the USOTC offers visitors the chance to discover US Olympic history through its indoor and outdoor exhibitions and installations. Walking tours are conducted daily.

Index

ABOUT THE AUTHOR

As the daughter of a track coach in Auburn, Alabama, Karen Rosen grew up holding the tape at the finish line. She attended her first Olympic Games in Montreal, Canada, in 1976 on a family vacation and worked for ABC at the 1984 Los Angeles Games. Rosen has covered every Olympics since 1992 as a journalist, including those in Barcelona, Spain, where her father, Mel, was the US men's track coach.